P

Sacagawea
and the Bravest Deed

written by
Stephen Krensky

illustrated by
Diana Magnuson

Aladdin

New York   London   Toronto   Sydney   Singapore

First Aladdin edition June 2002

Text copyright © 2002 by Stephen Krensky

Illustrations copyright © 2002 by Diana Magnuson

ALADDIN PAPERBACKS

An imprint of Simon & Schuster Children's Publishing Division

1230 Avenue of the Americas

New York, NY 10020

READY-TO-READ is a registered trademark of Simon & Schuster.

Book design by Lisa Vega

The text for this book was set in 17 Point Utopia.

Printed in the United States of America

2 4 6 8 10 9 7 5 3 1

Library of Congress Cataloging-in-Publication Data

available from the Library of Congress

ISBN 0-689-84803-X (Aladdin pbk.)

ISBN 0-689-85145-6 (Aladdin Library Edition)

Grass Maiden, who would one day
be called Sacagawea,
stared up at the great
Shoshone medicine tipi.

A curl of smoke drifted out the top.
She could hear much shouting
from inside.
"Grass Maiden," said her friend
Little Bird,
"what do you think is happening?"

Grass Maiden let out a sigh.
"The boys are telling stories
of their best hunts and
bravest deeds,"
she said.

"I would like the chance to hunt,"
said Little Bird.
"I would like the chance to be brave,"
said Grass Maiden.

Grass Maiden returned
to her family's tipi.
Her mother and grandmother
were busy grinding sunflower
seeds into flour.

"I am glad you are back,
  Grass Maiden," said Mother.
"We need more wood for the fire."
"I will come with you, Grass Maiden,"
  said Grandmother.
"Take my wooden knife," said Mother.
"It may help with the cutting."

As Grass Maiden and Grandmother
climbed into the hills, Grass Maiden
could see far across the valley.
But the sun was up higher.
It could see farther still.
"Someday," said Grass Maiden,
"I want to follow the sun on it's
journey across the sky."

Grass Maiden and her grandmother
gathered up wood
until their arms were full.
"It is time to start back,"
said Grandmother.

As they made their way
down the hillside,
Grass Maiden heard a rumbling noise
above them.
She looked up to see a boulder
rolling down the steep slope.

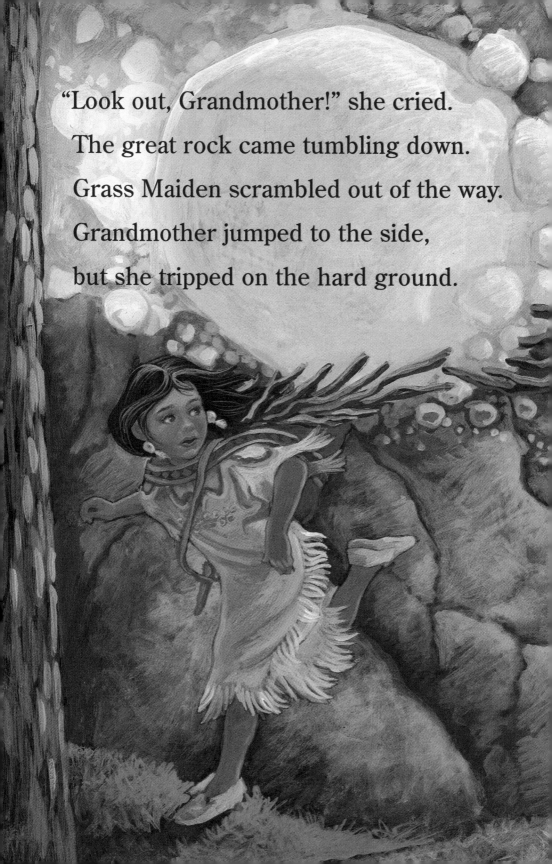

"Look out, Grandmother!" she cried.

The great rock came tumbling down.

Grass Maiden scrambled out of the way.

Grandmother jumped to the side,

but she tripped on the hard ground.

The boulder crashed down,
rolling past Grandmother
to rest against a rotting log.

"Grandmother!" said Grass Maiden.

"Are you all right?"

Grandmother sat up slowly.

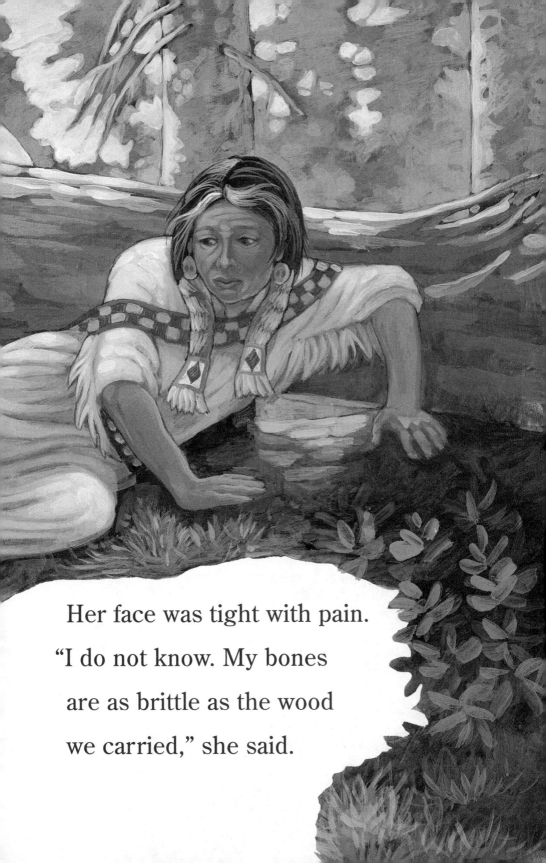

Her face was tight with pain.
"I do not know. My bones
are as brittle as the wood
we carried," she said.

R-a-a-t-t-l-l-e!

Grass Maiden turned quickly.
There, along the path,
a large rattlesnake
was slithering out of the log.
It had been sleeping there
until the boulder had
awakened it.

19

The snake was angry,
and Grandmother was right in its path.
"Run, Grandmother!" cried
Grass Maiden.

Grandmother tried to stand,
but sharp pains shot through her leg.
"I cannot," she said.
"My ankle is broken."

The snake was coiling up,
ready to strike.

Grass Maiden scooped up a stone
and threw it at the snake's head.

Thud! The snake fell, stunned.

Grass Maiden darted forward
with her mother's knife,
striking the snake.
Finally, the snake lay still.

"You have saved my life,"
said Grandmother.
"You did not run away.
It was a brave thing to do.

Now, you must help me, Grass Maiden.

We must leave the wood for later.

I cannot walk alone."

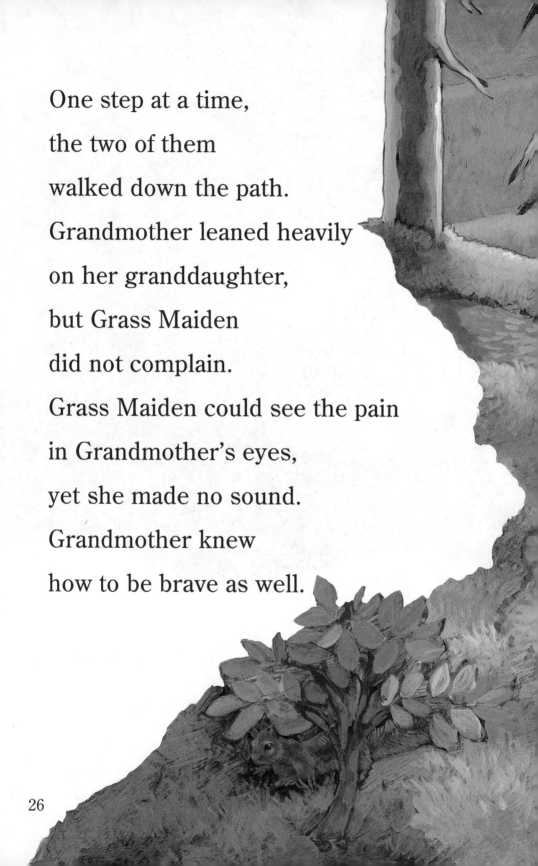

One step at a time,
the two of them
walked down the path.
Grandmother leaned heavily
on her granddaughter,
but Grass Maiden
did not complain.
Grass Maiden could see the pain
in Grandmother's eyes,
yet she made no sound.
Grandmother knew
how to be brave as well.

When they got back to camp,

Mother took care of Grandmother.

"I must go back for the wood,"

said Grass Maiden.

"It will be dark soon," Mother told her.

"I know the way," said Grass Maiden.

"I will not get lost."

"Very well," said Mother.

As Grass Maiden returned
to the path, the sun was setting.
She looked at the blaze
of colors and smiled.
"Someday, I will follow you," she said.
"To see where you go
when the day is done."

This book is based on a story about Sacagawea, a young Shoshone woman who later accompanied the explorers Meriwether Lewis and William Clark on their journey across the Louisiana Purchase. The timeline below identifies important events in her life.

1786   Born in present-day western Montana or eastern Idaho.

1799   Captured by band of Hidatsa Indians. Gains the name of Sacagawea, meaning "Bird Woman."

1804   Sold to the French-Canadian trapper Toussaint Charbonneau. He soon marries her.

1805   In February, gives birth to a son.

1805   In April, Sacagawea and her family go with Lewis and Clark traveling west across the Louisiana Purchase.

1805   In August, the expedition comes across Sacagawea's former tribe. She is briefly reunited with her brother, who now leads the tribe.

1804   Sacagawea stays with the expedition to the Pacific coast and back to North Dakota. Lewis and Clark Expedition ends in St. Louis.

1809   Sacagawea visits St. Louis, leaves her son to be educated by William Clark.

1812   Sacagawea dies in Fort Manuel, Dakota Territory. (Some sources claim she died much later, in 1884, on a Shoshone reservation.)